stuffed

in the middle

52 box mix treats with a surprise inside

Happy Baking Meredith!

jmety

Heaber

Printed in the United States of America
First printing, 2014

Haber, Holly TenEyck & Metz, Julie Connor
Stuffed in the Middle: 52 Box Mix Treats with a Surprise Inside

ISBN 978-0-9862918-2-1

Photographs by Julie Connor Metz
Edited by Cynthia TenEyck and Joan Connor

DEDICATIONS
To my amazing husband who encourages me at all times, even when I change my mind every couple of weeks. To my wonderful children who "endure" eating cupcakes every week and give me great feedback. —HTH

For my beloved family and cupcake tasters, who chase dreams with me and reflect the light. –JCM

ACKNOWLEDGEMENTS
With gratitude, to our families and friends who dropped what they were doing and helped us troubleshoot, taste and edit, particularly: Tony, techie guru Franki, Anthony & Emma Haber; sister Cynthia & niece Indigo TenEyck, Chris Hylen; mom Judy George; dad "the pie maker" Lynn TenEyck; Marie, Paul, Cameron & Brianna Boardman; Tony & Mary Haber; Laura, Sam, Angela & Lucas Haber; Matt, Hannah & Genevieve Metz; mom and dad, Joan & Denny Connor; baker Sandra Metz; 1K cookie baker & farmer Sally Klitz; sister Jill Connor; gardener Christy Bockmann; Christy & Tony Serniotti; The Conaway Family; The Hauss Family; Sheila Trumbo; June & Doc Nakamura-Foster; Tristen Leck; Nora Stevens; Lars D.H. Hedbor, Jennifer Mendenhall – and sometimes our dogs, Scarlett and Summit. Thanks to Alia Habib, who was the first agent to say we had a great concept and should write a blog; her feedback was validating.

VISIT US ONLINE
Blog: www.stuffedinthemiddle.com
Facebook: www.facebook.com/stuffedinthemiddle
Julie Metz Photography: www.gingersnap.smugmug.com

stuffed
in the middle

52 box mix treats with a surprise inside

Today's families are as busy as ever. Many of us appreciate the convenience of a box mix, but still want to create something special when we have a little time to bake. In this cookbook, we rely on some great shortcuts. What makes our recipes unique are the tricks and techniques we share for adding a surprise inside – Stuffed in the Middle.

You can make quick treats with a gourmet look at home. We've also included more than a dozen homemade recipes that we paired with 52 weeks of ideas for every season. Many recipes here take less than half an hour to prepare from start to finish.

We share our history when we share stories, like those told in the family cookbooks created for us. For 18 months, we baked, developed recipes, adjusted homemade favorites and shared lots of cupcakes... and laughter. As you enter these pages, we hope you'll embrace that spirit of joy.

Julie, Holly & Summit

Along the way, we personally learned a bit more about our food heritages. For example, we pulled flavor combinations from the weathered recipe cards of our grandmothers, mothers and fathers. We found answers to these and other questions: Why do cake box mixes rock? Why do we eat cheese with apple pie? How can we get away with eating raw cookie dough without getting food poisoning?

We invite you to trace your own foodie story, and discover how that history shapes the tastes that comfort you.

Warmly,
Julie & Holly

Download a free QR code reader app on your cell phone to access our video instructions (above).

TOOLS

Cupcake pan

Cupcake liners

2-inch cookie scoop

Apple/cupcake corer

Pastry bag
OR *resealable plastic bag*

1M decorator tip

RULES

1. Always use a cupcake liner with cupcakes, which gives them stability when coring the centers.

2. Use a 2-inch cookie scoop to fill cupcake liners two-thirds full.

*3. We bake all of our cupcakes **for only 18 minutes** so that they don't dry out. We note other bake times on non-cupcake recipes.*

*4. You don't need to put a decorator's tip into your **filling** bag unless the bag will also be used as a **filling/frosting**. Snip a 1/2-inch opening off of corner with scissors (every time with a disposable plastic bag, once only with a reusable pastry bag).*

*5. Always insert a 1M tip into the bag before spooning in **frosting** for decorating.*

Use leftover cupcake cores to create cake pops, following our TIP on page 76.

CORING

1. To create stuffed cupcakes, insert an apple or cupcake corer into the center of the cupcake, about 1-inch deep.

2. Remove cake from the center by pulling up, then set aside. If the corer doesn't pull out the cut center of the cupcake, remove it with a spoon.

PREPARE PASTRY BAG

1. Fold down the top of your pastry bag, and rest it in a glass.

2. With a 1M tip in the pastry bag, half fill bag with frosting.

3. Push the frosting down from the top of the bag.

4. Twist the bag so it closes just above the frosting.

5. Compress bag until the air is pressed out. This is called "burping" the bag.

6. Squeeze frosting into the cored cupcake center, 1/4 inch above the top.

HOW TO CIRCLE FROST

1. Gently place the frosting on the cupcake about a 1/4 inch in from the edge.

2. Using constant pressure, circle around the mound of filling in the center.

3. Start to climb the already piped-on frosting, circling up as you go.

4. To finish, stop pressure on the bag, push down slightly, and then pull the bag away.

'I CAN'T BELIEVE YOU WON'T GIVE ME YOUR SECRET'

Years ago, when I worked as an admin at a call center, I would make cakes for people in the office. I had one "taster" who asked for my secret of making my cake so moist. I told her, I bake the cake for about 5 minutes short of the directions, I let it cool in the pan for about 10 minutes, and then I pop it into the freezer. I decorate it when it's still frozen to lock in all the moisture.

She said, "Okay, but what's your recipe?" I told her I used a box mix. She glared at me ... literally, glared at me and said, "I was a baker for 12 years, and that was no box mix! I can't believe you won't give me your secret!" And she huffed away!

I was flabbergasted! Seriously?? If you ever get to know me, you'll know... I'll tell you anything! I just met you in the grocery store check-out line?? I'll know that you have two kids and how long your labor was. And you'll know that I have three kids and what I'm doing with all those boxes of cake mix that are in my buggy right now. That's right, I said buggy – not cart... I'm from the south y'all.

What I'm trying to say is, cake mixes ROCK!

 Holly

Winter

Week 1: Chocolate Orange Stuffed Cupcakes
Week 2: Gingerbread Caramel Stuffed Cupcakes
Week 3: Peppermint Mocha Stuffed Cupcakes
Week 4: Spiked Eggnog Stuffed Cupcakes
Week 5: Peach Bellini Stuffed Cupcakes
Week 6: Amaretto Stuffed Brownies
Week 7: Salted Caramel Pretzel Stuffed Cupcakes
Week 8: Cosmo Stuffed Cupcakes
Week 9: Crème Brûlée Stuffed Cupcakes
Week 10: Rocky Road Stuffed Cupcakes
Week 11: Bowl Game Chili Stuffed Muffins
Week 12: Zucchini Chocolate Stuffed Cupcakes
Week 13: Winter Wonderland Stuffed Cupcakes

Chocolate Orange Stuffed Cupcakes

Makes 18 cupcakes

BASE
1 chocolate cake box mix
Eggs, oil & water
   (per box directions)

FILLING
1/4 c. orange juice, pulp-free
1 (10 oz.) jar lemon curd
Zest of one orange

TOPPING
2 cans chocolate frosting
Dark chocolate candy orange
   OR 18 mandarin orange wedges
      2 sq. chocolate almond bark
      2 Tbsp. kosher salt

Garnish cupcakes with half of a dark chocolate orange slice or use a fresh mandarin section dipped in melted chocolate and sprinkled with salt. If chocolate begins to seize up (get crumbly), add 1 heaping tablespoon of shortening to warm chocolate, and stir well.

INSTRUCTIONS

1. Prepare chocolate cupcakes per box directions, **but only bake for 18 minutes.** Insert a toothpick to check for doneness; when it comes out clean, remove from oven. Let cool fully.

2. *While cupcakes bake, prepare filling & topping:*
Filling: Combine lemon curd, orange juice and orange zest. Place mixture in filling bag containing no tip. Set aside.
Topping: Heat 2 squares of chocolate almond bark in a microwave-safe dish according to package instructions. Peel mandarin orange and remove as much of the pith (white stringy stuff) as possible. Dip wedge about halfway into the melted chocolate and then place on a parchment-lined pan. Immediately sprinkle lightly with kosher salt. Let cool fully.

3. Core cooled cupcakes. Cut a 1/2-inch hole from corner of filling bag and fill cupcakes.

4. Insert 1M tip into chosen pastry bag. Fill bag with chocolate frosting, cut opening and circle frost cupcakes.

5. Place salted, chocolate-dipped mandarin section or half slice of dark chocolate candy orange on cupcake.

These taste like the best candied chocolate orange I ever ate on Christmas, only fresher. The zest in the filling pops in your mouth. Dip a mandarin orange segment into chocolate melted almond bark for a topper. ♥ *Julie*

Gingerbread Caramel Stuffed Cupcakes

Makes 18 cupcakes

BASE
1 gingerbread cake box mix
Eggs, oil & water *(per box directions)*

FILLING
1 can vanilla frosting
1/2 (17 oz.) jar butterscotch caramel topping
            (found on the ice cream aisle)

TOPPING
2 cans vanilla frosting
18 gingerbread man cookies
1/2 c. butterscotch caramel topping
1/2 c. powdered sugar, for dusting

INSTRUCTIONS

1. Prepare gingerbread cupcakes per box directions, **but only bake for 18 minutes.** Insert a toothpick to check for doneness; when it comes out clean, remove from oven. Let cool fully.

2. *While cupcakes bake, prepare filling:*
Mix 1/2 jar of butterscotch caramel topping with 1 can vanilla frosting. Place mixture in filling bag containing no tip. Set aside.

TIP: Unlike liners, cupcake wrappers are decorative papers that wrap around the outside of a baked cupcake. Prepare purchased cupcake wrap by inserting tab into slot. For best results, drop filled cupcake into wrapper from the top, then circle frost.

3. Core cooled cupcakes. Cut a 1/2-inch hole from corner of filling bag and fill cupcakes.

4. Insert 1M tip into chosen pastry bag. Fill bag with vanilla frosting, cut opening and circle frost cupcakes.

5. Using a fork, drizzle with caramel. When drizzling, hold fork high above cupcake to get a thin stream of topping and move back and forth for desired effect.

6. Place gingerbread man on cupcake. Using a sifter, sprinkle with powdered sugar.

Peppermint Mocha Stuffed Cupcakes

Makes 18 cupcakes

BASE
1 chocolate fudge cake box mix
6 tsp. instant coffee crystals
Eggs, oil & water *(per box directions)*

FILLING
1 can chocolate fudge frosting
2 Tbsp. peppermint coffee liqueur
   OR *Omit alcohol and add*
      3 drops peppermint extract.

TOPPING
2 cans chocolate fudge frosting
1 candy cane, crushed
White sparkling sugar

INSTRUCTIONS
1. Add coffee crystals to water and oil in chocolate fudge box mix, **but only bake for 18 minutes.** Insert a toothpick to check for doneness; when it comes out clean, remove from oven. Let cool fully.

2. *While cupcakes bake, prepare filling:*
Mix peppermint coffee liqueur with 1 can chocolate fudge frosting. Place mixture in filling bag containing no tip. Set aside.

For a non-alcoholic version, omit the peppermint coffee liqueur and replace with 3 drops of peppermint extract.

3. Core cooled cupcakes. Cut a 1/2-inch hole from corner of filling bag and fill cupcakes.

4. Insert 1M tip into chosen pastry bag. Fill bag with chocolate frosting, cut opening and circle frost cupcakes.

5. Sprinkle with crushed candy canes and white sparkling sugar.

Friends, a crackling fire and a little coffee peppermint to warm you and satisfy your sweet tooth? This is the perfect cocktail party cupcake, and easy as can be using a box mix and tasty add-ins. You get a lot of glamour for a little effort with our Peppermint Mocha Stuffed Cupcakes.
♥ Julie & Holly

Spiked Eggnog Stuffed Cupcakes

Makes 18 cupcakes

BASE
1 yellow cake box mix
Eggs, oil & water *(per box directions)*

FILLING
1 (5.1 oz.) box vanilla instant pudding
2 c. eggnog
1/4 c. rum
1/4 c. brandy
  OR *Omit alcohol, and increase*
    eggnog total to 2 ½ c.

TOPPING
2 cans vanilla frosting
Silver nonpareils
Fresh nutmeg
Holiday cupcake picks

MY FAVORITE PART
My favorite part about making cupcakes is the instant gratification of making something delicious and beautiful. I started making stuffed cupcakes after I tried one from a boutique cupcake bakery.
It looked so beautiful and tasted so good, that I wanted to make them myself.

So, through some research and fine-tuning, I started stuffing cupcakes. The bakery I went to probably bakes from scratch, but I'm not that kind of baker. I have three kids, and not a lot of time, so I use a box mix. I hear the collective gasp from the baking elite, but that's what they use in all the chain grocery store bakeries I've baked in – big bags of cake mix!
Plus, cake mixes make moister cupcakes.
♥ Holly

INSTRUCTIONS
1. Prepare yellow cupcakes per box directions, **but only bake for 18 minutes.** Insert a toothpick to check for doneness; when it comes out clean, remove from oven. Let cool fully.

2. *While cupcakes bake, prepare filling:*
Whisk together vanilla instant pudding with eggnog and alcohol. Place mixture in filling bag containing no tip. Set aside.

For a non-alcoholic version, *omit the rum and brandy, and increase the eggnog total to 2 ½ c.*

3. Core cooled cupcakes. Cut a 1/2-inch hole from corner of filling bag and fill cupcakes.

4. Insert 1M tip into chosen pastry bag. Fill bag with vanilla frosting, cut opening and circle frost cupcakes.

5. Garnish with silver nonpareils, freshly grated nutmeg and holiday cupcake picks.

These are some of our favorite holiday cupcakes yet. Who doesn't love eggnog during the holidays? Now add a little rum, brandy, fresh nutmeg, et voilà – a beautiful addition to any holiday table.

19

Peach Bellini Stuffed Cupcakes

Makes 18 cupcakes

BASE
1 white cake box mix
Eggs, oil & water
   (per box directions)

FILLING
1 (6 oz.) box peach gelatin
2 c. boiling water
1 c. ginger ale
1 c. Moscato d'Asti
   OR *Omit alcohol, and increase
       ginger ale total to 2 c.*

TOPPING
2 cans vanilla frosting
Silver & gold sprinkles

Have a little bubbly in your New Year's dessert.

INSTRUCTIONS

1. Prepare white cupcakes per box directions, **but only bake for 18 minutes.** Insert a toothpick to check for doneness; when it comes out clean, remove from oven. Let cool fully.

2. *While cupcakes bake, prepare filling:*
Mix gelatin with boiling water and stir until dissolved. Replace the cold water with ginger ale and Moscato d'Asti (or champagne). Refrigerate gelatin filling until fully set. Overnight is best.

For a non-alcoholic version, *omit the Moscato d'Asti, and increase the ginger ale total to 2 c.*

3. Core cooled cupcakes. Using a corer, core out a piece of prepared peach gelatin from the pan. Slide out of apple corer into the cored cupcake.

4. Insert 1M tip into chosen pastry bag. Fill bag with vanilla frosting, cut opening and circle frost cupcakes.

5. Top cupcakes with silver and gold sprinkles.

I'm not crazy about champagne (I know, I know — what's wrong with me??) but I love the sweet, sweet taste of Moscato d'Asti; add it to peach nectar and you have a Peach Bellini, my very favorite drink for New Year's Eve! Here's our version of Peach Bellini Stuffed Cupcakes to share with your guests at your next New Year's Eve party.
♥ Holly

21

Amaretto Stuffed Brownies

Makes 12 brownies

BASE
1 brownie box mix
Eggs, oil & water *(per box directions)*

FILLING
1 (12.5 oz.) can almond pastry filling
2 Tbsp. amaretto

TOPPING
2 cans milk chocolate frosting
Gold sugar pearls
Gold sparkling sugar
Sliced almonds

INSTRUCTIONS
1. For this recipe, bake brownies in a cupcake pan. Prepare brownie mix per box directions, **but bake 26-30 minutes**. Insert a toothpick to check for doneness; when it comes out clean, remove from oven. Let cool fully.

2. *While cupcakes bake, prepare filling:*
Open can of almond pastry filling, and stir in amaretto. Place mixture in filling bag containing no tip. Set aside.

For a non-alcoholic version, omit alcohol and just use almond pastry filling.

3. Core cooled brownies. Cut a 1/2-inch hole from corner of filling bag and fill cupcakes.

4. Insert 1M tip into chosen pastry bag. Fill bag with milk chocolate frosting, cut opening and circle frost cupcakes.

5. Sprinkle with gold sparkling sugar and gold sugar pearls, and top with two almond slices.

BLOG Q & A

Q: Which size pastry bag do you use?
Okay here is a Stuffed in the Middle question: I know it says a size 1M decorating tip (which was so helpful because who knew there were so many.) But what size frosting bag, as there are disposable ones which say they are 12" and the reusable ones with sizes 10" 12" 14" and 16"?

Is it useful to have the coupling for the 1M decorating tip, or is that just one more thing to have to wash? Maybe you only need that if you are changing tips, which the simple swirl frosting doesn't require. I suppose if a person doesn't do this too often, maybe the disposable frosting bags are the way to go. I have to go look in my archives from when I took a cake decorating class and see if I still have some of the tips. If I remember correctly, I rolled the frosting bag from parchment paper.
– Joan, Omaha, Neb.

A: You can use any size bag that you want.
Great question! I prefer using the bags that are a little larger so I don't have to keep refilling them. However, for a new pastry-bag user, the smaller might be better because your hands don't need to be as strong. I also cut the bags to fit the tip, and I don't use a coupler. You'd have to buy a larger coupler than they usually sell at your local craft store, and you only really need it if you are changing the tip for a different look.
♥ Holly

Salted Caramel Pretzel Stuffed Cupcakes
Makes 18 cupcakes

BASE
1 chocolate cake box mix
Eggs, oil, water *(per box directions)*
1 c. crushed mini pretzels
4 Tbsp. butter, melted

FILLING
1 (17 oz.) jar butterscotch caramel topping
     (found in the ice cream aisle)

TOPPING
2 cans white frosting
36 whole mini pretzels
Crushed mini pretzels

INSTRUCTIONS
1. Using a rolling pin, finely crush 1 c. of mini pretzels inside a closed resealable plastic bag. Place melted butter in a bowl; stir in crushed pretzels until completely coated. Mixture should resemble crumbs. Firmly press 1 Tbsp. of pretzel butter mixture into the bottom of each cupcake liner with the back of a spoon.

2. In a separate bowl, prepare chocolate cupcake batter per box directions. Top pretzel mixture with batter and place in oven, *but only bake for 18 minutes.* Insert a toothpick to check for doneness; when it comes out clean, remove from oven. Let cool fully.

3. Core cooled cupcakes. Fill each cored cupcake with 1 Tbsp. butterscotch caramel topping per cupcake.

4. Insert 1M tip into chosen pastry bag. Fill bag with vanilla frosting, cut opening and circle frost cupcakes.

5. Sprinkle with crushed pretzels and two whole mini pretzels.

Cosmo Stuffed Cupcakes

Makes 18 cupcakes

The combination of lime, cranberry and vanilla vodka stuffed in the center of these adorable cupcakes makes them taste just like a Cosmo. Garnish them with pink sparkling sugar and a lime wedge.

BASE
1 white cake box mix
Eggs, oil & water *(per box directions)*

FILLING
1 (14 oz.) can cranberry sauce, jellied
1/2 (10 oz.) jar lime curd
2 Tbsp. vanilla vodka
  OR *Omit alcohol and add 2 Tbsp. vanilla extract*

TOPPING
2 cans vanilla frosting
Pink sparkling sugar
Thinly sliced lime wedge

INSTRUCTIONS
1. Prepare white cupcakes per box directions, **but only bake for 18 minutes.** Insert a toothpick to check for doneness; when it comes out clean, remove from oven. Let cool fully.

2. *While cupcakes bake, prepare filling:*
Combine cranberry sauce, lime curd and vanilla vodka. Place mixture in filling bag containing no tip. Set aside.

For a non-alcoholic version, *replace vodka with 2 Tbsp. vanilla extract*

3. Core cooled cupcakes. Cut a 1/2-inch hole from corner of filling bag and fill cupcakes.

4. Insert 1M tip into chosen pastry bag. Fill bag with vanilla frosting, cut opening and circle frost cupcakes.

5. Garnish with pink sparkling sugar and lime wedge.

Crème Brûlée Stuffed Cupcakes

Makes 18 cupcakes

BASE
1 yellow cake box mix
Eggs, oil & water *(per box directions)*

FILLING
1 (5.1 oz.) box instant vanilla pudding
2 c. heavy whipping cream, liquid
1/2 c. milk

TOPPING
1 (12 oz.) tub whipped topping,
        thawed
Candied sugar *(See facing page.)*

INSTRUCTIONS
1. Prepare yellow cupcakes per box directions, **but only bake for 18 minutes.** Insert a toothpick to check for doneness; when it comes out clean, remove from oven. Let cool fully.

2. *While cupcakes bake, prepare filling:*
Stir together pudding mix, whipping cream and milk. Pudding will be thick. Place mixture in filling bag containing no tip. Set aside.

3. Core cooled cupcakes. Cut a 1/2-inch hole from corner of filling bag and fill cupcakes.

4. Insert 1M tip into chosen pastry bag. Fill bag with whipped topping, cut opening and circle frost cupcakes. Garnish with candied sugar.

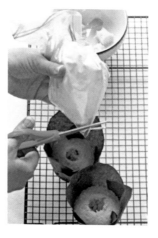

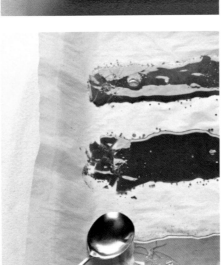

CANDIED SUGAR

1 c. sugar – granulated, raw or turbinado

1. Pour sugar on parchment paper and spread into a thin layer.

2. Place in oven set to Broil high. Broil, watching constantly, for about 5 minutes. When sugar turns to liquid and starts to brown, remove from oven. Let cool until hardened.

3. Using the back of a spoon, break sugar into small pieces, and *carefully* place on the cupcakes.

Rocky Road Stuffed Cupcakes

Makes 18 cupcakes

BASE
1 chocolate cake box mix
Eggs, oil & water *(per box directions)*

FILLING
1 (5.1 oz.) box instant chocolate pudding
2 c. milk
1/2 c. mini chocolate chips

TOPPING
2 cans milk chocolate frosting
1/2 c. micro-mini marshmallows
1/2 c. mini chocolate chips
1/2 c. chopped pecans or walnuts
18 pecan halves

INSTRUCTIONS

1. Prepare chocolate cupcakes per box directions, **but only bake for 18 minutes.** Insert a toothpick to check for doneness; when it comes out clean, remove from oven. Let cool fully.

2. *While cupcakes bake, prepare filling:*
Prepare chocolate instant pudding per pie filling instructions on the box. Add 1/2 c. mini chocolate chips to pudding, and stir until combined. Place mixture in filling bag containing no tip. Set aside.

3. Core cooled cupcakes. Cut a 1/2-inch hole from corner of filling bag and fill cupcakes.

4. Insert 1M tip into chosen pastry bag. Fill bag with chocolate frosting, cut opening and circle frost cupcakes.

5. Combine mini marshmallows, mini chocolate chips and nuts, creating a rocky road mixture. Sprinkle liberally onto cupcakes.

Bowl Game Chili Stuffed Muffins

Makes 16 muffins

We love easy, tasty party nibbles. Football fan or not, it doesn't get much easier than this: corn bread mix + a can of chili + sour cream + cilantro = a snack for 16 made in 20 minutes.
Adapt this in a variety of ways, to taste: substitute veggie chili; diced jalapeños incorporated into the muffin batter for heat; scallions on top; shredded cheese, etc. ♥ *Julie*

BASE
2 (8.5 oz.) corn muffin box mixes
Egg & water *(per box directions)*

FILLING
1 (15 oz.) can chili

TOPPING
1 c. sour cream
1 bunch cilantro

INSTRUCTIONS
1. Prepare and bake muffins per box directions. Let cool.

2. Warm chili in covered microwave-safe bowl for 1 minute on high.

3. Core muffins and spoon in warmed chili.

4. Top with 1 tsp. sour cream and a single cilantro leaf per muffin.

Zucchini Chocolate Stuffed Cupcakes

Makes 18 cupcakes

Hide the veggies: The kids won't notice, and the adults will enjoy the rich flavor of these tasty cupcakes.

BASE
1 chocolate cake box mix
Eggs & oil *(per box directions)*
2 c. shredded zucchini *(replaces water)*
1 c. mini chocolate chips

FILLING
1 can vanilla frosting

TOPPING
2 cans chocolate frosting
18 fresh lemon thyme buds *(optional)*
Chocolate chips

INSTRUCTIONS

1. Grate fresh zucchini. Do not drain; moisture from the zucchini replaces the water listed on the box mix.

2. Add zucchini to box mix and prepare chocolate cupcakes per remaining directions, adding in mini chocolate chips. ***Only bake for 18 minutes.*** Insert a toothpick to check for doneness; when it comes out clean, remove from oven. Let cool fully.

3. Core cooled cupcakes. Place vanilla frosting in filling bag containing no tip. Cut a 1/2-inch hole from corner of filling bag and fill cupcakes.

4. Insert 1M tip into chosen pastry bag. Fill bag with chocolate frosting, cut opening and circle frost cupcakes.

5. Sprinkle with chocolate chips and garnish with lemon thyme.

My grandma always had an extra zucchini, or three, to send home with us after a visit to the farm. Hence, our family cookbook has several dessert recipes that include the ingredient. Since becoming a mom, I've used zucchini in quick breads that my kids now enjoy. ♥ Julie

Winter Wonderland Stuffed Cupcakes

Makes 18 cupcakes

My daughter requested Winter Wonderland for her birthday theme, and asked for mint and white chocolate chip stuffed cupcakes. Holly imagined how we might use cloches and micro-mini marshmallows to create a whimsical treat resembling a snow globe.
Don't forget the trees! ♥ Julie

BASE
1 vanilla cake box mix
Eggs, oil and water *(per box directions)*

FILLING
6 c. powdered sugar
8 drops peppermint extract
3/4 tsp. vanilla extract
1/3 c. butter, softened
1/3 c. milk
1/2 c. white chocolate chips

TOPPING
2 cans vanilla frosting
White sparkling sugar
Sugar pearls
Candy snowflake sprinkles
Blue sparkling sugar
1 (3 oz.) jar micro-mini marshmallows

INSTRUCTIONS

1. Prepare vanilla cupcakes per box directions, **but only bake for 18 minutes.** Insert a toothpick to check for doneness; when it comes out clean, remove from oven. Let cool fully.

2. *While cupcakes bake, prepare filling:*
Use an electric mixer to cream together peppermint extract, vanilla extract, milk and softened butter. Slowly add in powdered sugar to creamed butter mixture. Mixture will resemble frosting once combined. Using a spatula or spoon, stir in white chocolate chips. Place mixture in filling bag containing no tip. Set aside.

3. Core cooled cupcakes. Cut a 1/2-inch hole from corner of filling bag and fill cupcakes.

4. Insert 1M tip into chosen pastry bag. Fill bag with plain vanilla frosting, cut opening and circle frost cupcakes.

5. Sprinkle with white sparkling sugar, sugar pearls, candy snowflake sprinkles or blue sparkling sugar.

SUGAR CONE TREES

1. Place pastry bag containing tip (#19) against the sugar cone, about 1 inch from the bottom of the cone. Squeeze pastry bag until frosting comes out, then gently pull away from the cone and release pressure from bag.

2. Continue to pipe around the bottom of the sugar cone, completing a circle of branches. When the first layer is done, move up about a 1/2 inch, and begin piping branches so they are spaced in between the branches below (think checkerboard pattern). Continue to pipe branches until you reach the top, and the tip of the cone is covered. Top tree with sifted powdered sugar, white sparkling sugar or silver pearls.

Spring

Lemon Chiller Stuffed Cupcakes

Makes 18 cupcakes

BASE
1 white cake box mix
Eggs, oil & water *(per box directions)*

FILLING
1 (10 oz.) jar lemon curd
  OR *homemade lemon curd, page 55*

TOPPING
2 cans vanilla frosting
1 box lemon semi-soft candies
1/2 c. powdered sugar

INSTRUCTIONS
1. Prepare white cupcakes per box directions, **but only bake for 18 minutes.** Insert a toothpick to check for doneness; when it comes out clean, remove from oven. Let cool fully.

2. Place lemon curd in filling bag containing no tip. Set aside.

3. Core cooled cupcakes. Cut a 1/2-inch hole from corner of filling bag and fill cupcakes.

4. Insert 1M tip into chosen pastry bag. Fill bag with plain vanilla frosting, cut opening and circle frost cupcakes.

5. Place a lemon candy on each cupcake and sprinkle with sifted powdered sugar.

Chocolate Strawberry Stuffed Jelly Roll

Serves 10

BASE
1 angel food cake box mix
Water *(per box directions)*

FILLING
2 c. frozen strawberries, whole
1 (3.4 oz.) box cheesecake instant pudding
1 (12 oz.) tub whipped topping
1 can milk chocolate frosting
1 drop gel pink food coloring *(optional)*

TOPPING
1 c. mini chocolate chips
1½ Tbsp. shortening

INSTRUCTIONS
1. Combine cake mix and water per box directions.

2. Line 12½" x 17" jellyroll pan with waxed paper and spread batter into pan.

3. Place pan in oven and cook at 350 degrees for 25 minutes. Remove and let cool for 5 minutes. *(See facing page for filling & assembly directions.)*

4. Refrigerate until serving. To serve, cut 1-inch slices from the end, like a loaf of bread. This highlights the swirl.

Strawberry filling makes enough for two jelly rolls.

HOW TO MAKE A JELLY ROLL

INSTRUCTIONS

1. Place a tea towel on the counter and sift 1/2 c. powdered sugar onto it.

2. *While cake bakes, prepare filling:*
Microwave frozen strawberries on high for 1 minute. Mash with fork. Combine with pudding, whipped topping and food coloring (optional). Set aside.

3. Remove cake from oven; after 5 minutes, flip onto towel. Gently peel back waxed paper, and discard. Roll the tea towel into the cake, and cool for 1 hour.

4. Unroll cake. Microwave chocolate frosting on high for 1 minute. Spread frosting 1/2 inch from edge. Once cooled, spread half of strawberry filling on top, 1 inch from edge. Re-roll cake back into log shape, minus the towel.

5. Combine chocolate chips and shortening and heat in microwave. *(See instruction 3, page 76.)* Using a fork, drizzle jelly roll with chocolate. Refrigerate before serving.

Strawberry Stuffed Heart Cakes

Makes 4 cakes

BASE

1 store-bought, sliced pound cake
   OR 1 pound cake box mix, per box directions

FILLING

1 (12 oz.) tub whipped topping
1 (18 oz.) jar strawberry jam
2 lbs. strawberries

TOPPING

4 whole strawberries
4 fresh mint sprigs

INSTRUCTIONS

1. Using a medium heart-shaped cookie cutter, cut shapes from each slice of pound cake.

2. Place one heart-shaped slice of cake on a plate. Spoon on a layer of strawberry jam. Insert 1M tip into chosen pastry bag. Fill bag with whipped topping and cut opening. Top jam by piping stars (See *TIP* below). Place sliced strawberries on top of whipped topping, with the widest part toward the center, allowing the strawberry points to slightly overhang the edge of cake.

3. Place a second heart-shaped cake slice on top of first layer. Pipe on more whipped topping and place a fanned strawberry on top. Place a sprig of mint next to strawberry.

TIP: To create stars between layers, squeeze bag briefly, stop pressure, then pull straight up.

MAKE A FANNED STRAWBERRY TOPPER

1. Cut the leaves off of a strawberry.

2. Slice strawberry vertically in equal-sized slices, similar to fringe, leaving base uncut.

3. Gently press on strawberry while fanning the slices and place on top of your favorite dessert.

Red Velvet Valentine Stuffed Cupcakes

Makes 18 cupcakes

BASE
1 red velvet cake box mix
Eggs, oil & water *(per box directions)*

FILLING/FROSTING
Homemade Cream Cheese Frosting
1/2 c. cream cheese, softened
1/2 c. butter, softened
2 Tbsp. vanilla extract
8 c. sifted powdered sugar

TOPPING
1 jar nonpareils
Plastic heart picks

INSTRUCTIONS
1. Prepare red velvet cupcakes per box directions, **but only bake for 18 minutes.** Insert a toothpick to check for doneness; when it comes out clean, remove from oven. Let cool fully.

2. *While cupcakes bake, prepare filling/frosting:*
With a mixer, cream together vanilla, softened cream cheese and butter. Slowly add sifted powdered sugar. Beat until smooth. Insert 1M tip into chosen pastry bag. Fill bag with filling/frosting and cut opening.

3. Core cooled cupcakes and pipe in filling/frosting. Use same bag to circle frost cupcakes.

4. Sprinkle with nonpareils and insert heart picks.

Rainbow Surprise Stuffed Cupcakes

Makes 18 cupcakes

BASE
1 vanilla cake box mix
Eggs, oil & water *(per box directions)*

FILLING
2 c. chocolate-covered sunflower seeds

TOPPING
2 cans vanilla frosting
1¼ c. chocolate-covered sunflower seeds
18 gold foil chocolate coins

INSTRUCTIONS
1. Prepare vanilla cupcakes per box directions, **but only bake for 18 minutes.** Insert a toothpick to check for doneness; when it comes out clean, remove from oven. Let cool fully.

2. Core cooled cupcakes and insert 1 tsp. sunflower seeds per cupcake.

3. Insert 1M tip into chosen pastry bag. Fill bag with plain vanilla frosting, cut opening and circle frost cupcakes.

4. Garnish cupcakes with chocolate sunflower seeds and a gold foil chocolate coin.

The nuttiness and crunch of sunflower seeds pair well with this vanilla cupcake.

Grasshopper Cookie Stuffed Cupcakes

Makes 18 cupcakes

BASE
1 chocolate cake box mix
Eggs, oil & water *(per box directions)*
18 mint sandwich cookies

TOPPING
2 cans vanilla frosting
1/4 mint cookie per cupcake

FILLING
1 (8 oz.) tub whipped topping
1 (7 oz.) jar marshmallow crème
2 tsp. crème de menthe
    OR *Omit alcohol and add*
       3 drops peppermint extract
6 mint sandwich cookies, crushed
7 drops green food coloring

INSTRUCTIONS

1. Place a mint cookie in the bottom of your cupcake liners. Foil liners are best here. In a separate bowl, prepare chocolate cupcake batter per box directions. Top cookie with batter and place in oven, **but only bake for 18 minutes.** Insert a toothpick to check for doneness; when it comes out clean, remove from oven. Let cool fully.

2. *While cupcakes bake, prepare filling:*
Mix whipped topping, marshmallow crème, crème de menthe and add 7 drops of green food coloring. Place 6 cookies in a closed resealable plastic bag and crush with a rolling pin. Mix cookie crumbs into mint marshmallow mixture. Place mixture in filling bag containing no tip. Set aside.

For a non-alcoholic version, *replace crème de menthe with 3 drops peppermint extract.*

3. Core cooled cupcakes. Cut a 1/2-inch hole from corner of filling bag and fill cupcakes.

4. Insert 1M tip into chosen pastry bag. Fill bag with plain vanilla frosting, and cut an opening. Pipe one circle around the mint marshmallow filling. Add more filling so it mounds up above the frosting. *(See photo.)*

5. Cut a mint cookie into quarters. Place cookie piece on top of cupcake and sprinkle with crushed mint cookies.

My Irish Grandma, Mary, made a refrigerator grasshopper pie with a sandwich cookie crust. I still remember licking the crunchy cookies from my lips as a kid.

Today, whipped topping and marshmallow crème lighten the filling texture in our Grasshopper Cookie Stuffed Cupcakes. There is also a cookie surprise baked into the base.

♥ Julie

43

Chocolate Egg Stuffed Cupcakes

Makes 18 cupcakes

BASE
1 chocolate fudge cake box mix
Eggs, oil & water *(per box directions)*

FILLING
18 mini crème or chocolate eggs

TOPPING
2 cans white frosting
3 stripes green food coloring paste
18 mini chocolate bunnies
1 bag of jellybeans

Place an unwrapped mini chocolate bunny on top of the cupcake and surround with three jellybeans.

INSTRUCTIONS

1. Prepare chocolate cupcakes per box directions, **but only bake for 18 minutes.** Insert a toothpick to check for doneness; when it comes out clean, remove from oven. Let cool fully.

2. *While cupcakes bake, prepare frosting:*
Mix vanilla frosting with food coloring. Once thoroughly combined, place green frosting in a pastry bag containing a "grass" tip *(#133)* in place of standard 1M tip. Set aside.

3. Core cooled cupcakes and insert unwrapped chocolate egg. Place cupcake into fence cupcake wrap. Cut opening in pastry bag. Pipe on grass by placing decorating tip against the cupcake. Briefly squeeze the bag; stop squeezing and pull up and away quickly. Work in a circle from the outside cupcake. Work in a circle towards the center, filling in grass as you go.

4. Garnish with chocolate bunny and jellybeans

We've created these Chocolate Egg Stuffed Cupcakes, so that you're little "cupcake" is never without his or her own chocolate bunny.
♥ Holly

Raspberry Lemonade Stuffed Cupcakes

Makes 18 cupcakes

BASE
1 vanilla cake box mix
Eggs & oil *(per box directions)*
1/2 (12 oz.) can frozen lemonade
            concentrate *(substitute for water)*

FILLING
36 fresh raspberries

TOPPING
2 cans vanilla frosting
Zest of 2 lemons *(1 lemon per can of frosting)*
18 fresh raspberries
Fresh mint leaves
White sparkling sugar

INSTRUCTIONS
1. Replace all water in box mix directions with lemonade concentrate. Then prepare vanilla cupcakes per box directions, **but only bake for 18 minutes.** Insert a toothpick to check for doneness; when it comes out clean, remove from oven. Let cool fully.

2. *While cupcakes bake, prepare frosting:* Stir zest into the vanilla frosting. Insert 1M tip into chosen pastry bag. Fill bag with lemon-vanilla frosting.

3. Core cooled cupcakes and gently insert two whole raspberries per cupcake; cut opening in bag, and circle frost cupcakes.

4. Sprinkle with white sparkling sugar. Top with a fresh raspberry and a mint sprig.

WHEN LIFE GIVES YOU LEMONS

Recently, my son was leaving school for the day and found that the car parked next to his was so close, he was unable to open the door.

As an "early release" student, he knew it would probably be several hours before the owner would return. My son is over 6 ft. tall and has a 2-door car; he had to get creative.

Since he couldn't get in through the driver's side, he had to get in the passenger side and climb over the console. He tried to lean over it, but kept bumping his head on the roof. After a few whacks to his head, he thought: Well, I'll just turn on the car, open the sunroof and attempt to climb across.

When he swung his leg over the console, he bumped the windshield wiper lever. Washer fluid sprayed in his face, the windshield wipers start swishing and his radio was blasting, (because why would you turn it down?)

By now, he'd gathered quite a crowd of students and still hadn't made it to the driver's seat. He did eventually make it over and left a note for the other driver. It wasn't very nice, but it ended with: Love, Anthony.

In the spirit of the challenges we face everyday, I thought I'd make a lemon-themed cupcake.

When life gives you lemons...
♥ Holly

Carrot Spice Stuffed Cupcakes

Makes 18 cupcakes

BASE
1 carrot cake box mix
Eggs, oil & water *(per box directions)*

FILLING/FROSTING
3 cans cream cheese frosting
  OR *Prepare 1 recipe homemade cream cheese frosting recipe, page 40.*
2¼ tsp. nutmeg
2¼ tsp. cardamom
1/2 tsp. ginger

TOPPING
1 (6 oz.) bag pecan pieces
1 carrot, julienned
1 (2 oz.) jar crystallized ginger
5 gingersnap cookies
2 tsp. nutmeg

INSTRUCTIONS
1. Prepare carrot cupcakes per box directions, **but only bake for 18 minutes.** Insert a toothpick to check for doneness; when it comes out clean, remove from oven. Let cool fully.

2. *While cupcakes bake, make filling/frosting*: Combine cream cheese frosting with nutmeg, cardamom and ginger. Insert 1M tip into chosen pastry bag. Fill bag with filling/frosting and cut opening.

3. Core cooled cupcakes and pipe in filling/frosting. Use same bag to circle frost cupcakes.

4. Garnish with carrot, a 1/4 piece of gingersnap cookie, crystallized ginger, pecan pieces or grated nutmeg.

OPTIONAL ROLLED TOPPING TECHNIQUE
Gather small amount of pecan pieces in palm and pat in a circle around the frosting's outer edge.

We're always looking for a great dessert to serve after Easter dinner. Carrot cake, combined with the flavorful trifecta of cardamom, cinnamon and ginger, creates this sweet, spice-infused cupcake.

49

Hummingbird Stuffed Cupcakes

Makes 18 cupcakes

BASE
1 carrot cake box mix
Eggs, oil & water *(per box directions)*
1 ripe banana
1/2 c. canned pineapple, crushed
1/2 c. walnuts or pecans

FILLING/FROSTING
2 cans cream cheese frosting
   OR *Prepare 1 recipe homemade cream cheese frosting recipe, page 40.*

TOPPING
2 c. sweetened coconut, toasted

Toast the coconut and use it to make a "nest" for this cute little bird! Enjoy! ♥ Holly

INSTRUCTIONS
1. Empty crushed pineapple from can into a fine mesh strainer. Using the back of a spoon, press pineapple against the strainer to remove and discard as much juice as possible.

2. In mixing bowl, place 1 ripe banana (mash with a fork), strained pineapple, carrot cake box mix and nuts, plus ingredients listed on the box mix directions. Mix thoroughly. ***Only bake for 18 minutes.*** Insert a toothpick to check for doneness; when it comes out clean, remove from oven. Let cool fully.

3. *While cupcakes bake, prepare filling/frosting & topping:*
Filling/Frosting: Insert 1M tip into chosen pastry bag. Fill bag with cream cheese filling/frosting and cut opening.
Topping: Place coconut onto a parchment-lined pan, and toast for 3-5 minutes or until golden brown. Set aside to cool.

4. Core cooled cupcakes and pipe in filling/frosting. Use same bag to circle frost cupcakes.

5. Sprinkle with toasted coconut and top with a cupcake pick.

I love bird watching. I got my first little visitor – a Black-Capped Chickadee – in my window-mounted birdhouse and was inspired to create these Hummingbird Stuffed Cupcakes. We've made it easy by adding banana, pineapple and nuts to a carrot cake box mix.
♥ Holly

51

Aztec Chili Chocolate Stuffed Cupcakes

Makes 18 cupcakes

BASE
1 chocolate cake box mix
Eggs, oil & water *(per box directions)*
1 Tbsp. ground cinnamon

FILLING
1 can vanilla frosting
1 Tbsp. ground cinnamon

TOPPING
2 cans milk chocolate frosting
1 (3oz.) bar of chili chocolate
Harvest-colored sugar pearls

INSTRUCTIONS
1. Adding in 1 Tbsp. of ground cinnamon to the box mix, prepare chocolate cupcakes per box directions, **but only bake for 18 minutes.** Insert a toothpick to check for doneness; when it comes out clean, remove from oven. Let cool fully.

2. *While cupcakes bake, prepare filling:*
Stir cinnamon into vanilla frosting. Place mixture in filling bag containing no tip. Set aside.

3. Core cooled cupcakes. Cut a 1/2-inch hole from corner of filling bag and fill cupcakes.

4. Insert 1M tip into chosen pastry bag. Fill bag with plain chocolate frosting, cut opening and circle frost cupcakes.

5. With a zester, finely grate 1 sq. chili chocolate bar over frosted cupcakes. Top with diagonally halved square of chocolate and sugar pearls.

OK, these taste really good. We finely grated chili chocolate squares and sprinkled them on top of our Aztec Chili Chocolate Stuffed Cupcakes. You may be surprised by how the cinnamon and vanilla frosting stuffed in the center mellows the taste; think more cinnamon gum flavor at the finish than jalapeño hot.

Cadillac Margarita Stuffed Cupcakes

Makes 18 cupcakes

BASE
1 orange cake box mix
Eggs, oil & water *(per box directions)*

FILLING
1 recipe lime curd *(See facing page.)*
  OR *1 (10 oz.) jar lime curd*
1/2 tsp. tequila, *per cupcake*
  OR *Omit alcohol and add*
      1/2 tsp. orange juice, per cupcake

TOPPING
1 can vanilla frosting
Kosher salt
9 lime wedges, halved

INSTRUCTIONS
1. Prepare orange cupcakes per box directions, **but only bake for 18 minutes.** Insert a toothpick to check for doneness; when it comes out clean, remove from oven. Let cool fully.

2. *While cupcakes bake, prepare filling:*
Prepare lime curd filling per directions on facing page. Cool to room temperature and then refrigerate for 20 minutes.

3. Core cooled cupcakes. Pour 1/2 tsp. tequila into the center of each cored cupcake. Then insert filling with a spoon.

TIP: Adding the 1/2 tsp. of tequila or orange juice makes for a moister orange cake.

For a non-alcoholic version, omit the alcohol and substitute 1/2 tsp. orange juice.

4. Insert 1M tip into chosen pastry bag. Fill bag with plain vanilla frosting, cut opening and circle frost cupcakes.

5. Lightly sprinkle each cupcake with salt. Garnish with a halved lime wedge.

LIME CURD FILLING
1 c. sugar
3 eggs
1 c. lime juice
Zest of 3 limes
1 stick unsalted butter, melted
1 Tbsp. cornstarch
1 Tbsp. water

ORANGE CURD FILLING
Substitute 1 c. orange juice and the zest of 2 oranges. Garnish with an orange twist, orange zest or sliced orange candies.

LEMON CURD FILLING
Substitute 1 c. of lemon juice and the zest of 3 lemons. Garnish with lemon zest, white sparkling sugar or a lemon twist.

INSTRUCTIONS
1. In a medium saucepan, whisk together sugar and eggs until smooth. Stir in lime juice, lime zest and butter.

2. In a separate bowl, stir cornstarch into the water until it is completely dissolved. Set aside.
Cook lime mixture over medium heat on stove top for 5 minutes, whisking constantly. Whisk cornstarch mixture into lime mixture and continue to whisk while cooking for another 2 to 3 minutes, or until thick and bubbly.

3. Remove from heat and continue to stir for another minute or two. Let curd come to room temperature for about 10 minutes and then refrigerate until cool, about 2 hours.

4. Once curd is cool, spoon into cored cupcakes.

Blackberry Cream Stuffed Angel Food Cake

Serves 10

BASE
1 angel food cake box mix
Water *(per box directions)*

FILLING/DOLLOPS
1½ c. heavy whipping cream
5 blackberries, crushed
1½ Tbsp. sugar

TOPPING
2/3 c. blackberry preserves
Edible sugared flowers

In a hurry? Skip the pastry bag and spread filling between the layers of cake with a spatula. You can use a teaspoon to apply the dollops on top.

INSTRUCTIONS

1. Prepare and bake angel food cake per box directions, pouring into a long loaf pan *(5"W x 16"L x 4"D)*. Cake is done when the top is golden brown and cracks appear dry. Invert cake and let cool fully in the pan.

2. *While cake bakes, prepare filling:*
Using your mixer, pour 1 c. heavy whipping cream and 1 Tbsp. sugar into a bowl and whip until stiff peaks form. Gently fold in 5 crushed berries. Refrigerate filling until cake is completely cool. **For best results, assemble immediately before serving.**

3. Slice cooled cake lengthwise. Remove top layer of cake and set aside. Place two-thirds of the mixture into a pastry bag containing a 1M tip, and pipe blackberry filling onto cake in a zigzag motion. Gently replace top layer of cake; do not press down.

4. Place blackberry preserves into a microwave-safe measuring cup. Microwave on high for 1 minute, or until melted. Stir to eliminate any clumps. Pour over the top of the cake using the back of a spoon to spread.

5. Place remainder of filling in pastry bag containing 1M tip and make 5 small rosettes on the top of the cake by circling the tip while squeezing the pastry bag.

6. Garnish with berry whipped cream rosettes with organic, edible sugared flowers. *(See page 58.)*

Spending time together baking is a satisfying way to reconnect with mom. Simplify by using a box mix, and you can enjoy sugaring flowers together, drizzling blackberry jam and finessing whipped cream. It makes for an impressive, jeweled presentation. Prepare to "ooh"and "aah" over our Blackberry Cream Stuffed Angel Food Cake.
♥ Julie

SUGARED FLOWERS

INGREDIENTS
10 organic edible flowers *(in the produce department)*
1 egg white
1/2 c. superfine sugar
  OR granulated sugar blended in a grinder or food processor

TOOLS
A new, small paint brush

INSTRUCTIONS
1. Gently rinse edible flowers with water and pat dry with a paper towel. Let dry fully.

2. On a plate, gently paint flower front with egg whites. Place egg-white-side down into sugar. Paint the backside of the flower with egg white and then flip flower over. Gently dust off excess sugar.

3. Place sugared flowers in a foil-lined baking pan. Bake at 170 degrees for 40 minutes or until sugared flowers are completely dry.

Summer

S'mores Stuffed Cupcakes

Makes 18 cupcakes

BASE
1 chocolate cake box mix
Eggs, oil & water *(per box directions)*
1 c. graham cracker crumbs
1/2 stick butter, melted

FILLING
1 (7oz.) jar marshmallow crème

TOPPING
1 can milk chocolate frosting
18 large marshmallows
1 c. graham cracker crumbs
9 squares solid milk chocolate

INSTRUCTIONS

1. In a bowl, mix 1 c. graham cracker crumbs and melted butter together. Place 1 Tbsp. of the mixture into each cupcake liner; press down firmly with back of tablespoon.

2. In a separate bowl, prepare chocolate cupcake batter per box directions. Top graham cracker mixture with batter and place in oven, **but only bake for 18 minutes.** Insert a toothpick to check for doneness; when it comes out clean, remove from oven. Let cool fully.

3. Place marshmallow crème in filling bag containing no tip. Core cooled cupcakes. Cut a 1/2-inch hole from corner of filling bag and fill cupcakes.

4. Return baked and filled cupcakes to pan and place a large marshmallow on top. Place under the broiler, set on high. Toast about 3 minutes or until golden brown. Remove from oven and let cupcakes cool.

5. Insert 1M tip into chosen pastry bag. Fill bag with plain milk chocolate frosting, and cut an opening. Pipe one circle around the toasted marshmallow. Gather small amount of graham cracker crumbs in palm and pat in a circle around the frosting's outer edge. Garnish with a diagonally halved chocolate square.

S'mores are great at the beach and summer campouts. Re-create that taste memory any time of year with our S'mores Stuffed Cupcakes. The secret is baking in the graham crust, broiling the 'mallows and topping them with a piece of chocolate. Ooey, gooey, nom, nom.

Jam Stuffed Cupcakes

Makes 18 cupcakes

BASE
1 white cake box mix
Eggs, oil & water *(per box directions)*

FILLING
1 (17.5 oz.) jar raspberry or
blackberry jam

TOPPING
2 cans vanilla frosting
White sugar pearls
18 fresh raspberries or blackberries

INSTRUCTIONS
1. Prepare white cupcakes per box
directions, **but only bake for 18
minutes.** Insert a toothpick to
check for doneness; when it comes
out clean, remove from oven. Let
cool fully.

2. Place raspberry or blackberry
jam in filling bag containing no tip.
Set aside.

3. Core cooled cupcakes. Cut a 1/2-
inch hole from corner of filling bag
and fill cupcakes.

4. Insert 1M tip into chosen pastry
bag. Fill bag with plain vanilla
frosting, cut opening and circle
frost cupcakes.

5. Garnish with sugar pearls and a
fresh berry.

Zesty Stuffed Cupcakes

Makes 18 cupcakes

I'm a sucker for anything tart. The zest in the curd offsets the sweet vanilla frosting in a refreshing way. It's your own little dessert, hands off! These also freeze well.
♥ Julie

BASE
1 vanilla cake box mix
Eggs, oil & water *(per box directions)*

FILLING
1 (10 oz.) jar lime, orange or lemon curd
   OR homemade curd (See page 55.)

TOPPING
2 cans vanilla frosting
Lemon zest, lime slice
   or orange zest or candies
1 c. graham cracker crumbs
White sparkling sugar

INSTRUCTIONS
1. Prepare vanilla cupcakes per box directions, **but only bake for 18 minutes.** Insert a toothpick to check for doneness; when it comes out clean, remove from oven. Let cool fully.

2. Place curd in filling bag containing no tip. Set aside.

3. Core cooled cupcakes. Cut a 1/2-inch hole from corner of filling bag and fill cupcakes.

4. Insert 1M tip into chosen pastry bag. Fill bag with plain vanilla frosting, cut opening and circle frost cupcakes.
Gather small amount of graham cracker crumbs in palm and pat in a circle around the frosting's outer edge.

5. Garnish with zest, white sparkling sugar, fruit twist or orange candy.

Ice Cream Stuffed Cupcake Cones

Makes 12 cones

BASE
1 confetti cake box mix
Eggs, oil & water *(per box directions)*
1 dozen flat-bottomed ice cream cones

FILLING
1/2 gallon of your favorite ice cream

TOPPING
1 (14 oz.) can aerosol whipped cream
12 maraschino cherries
Sprinkles
Your favorite ice cream toppings

INSTRUCTIONS

1. Prepare confetti cupcake mix per box instructions. Place empty ice cream cones upright in a cupcake pan. Fill ice cream cones two-thirds full with cake batter, **but only bake for 18 minutes.** Insert a toothpick to check for doneness; when it comes out clean, remove from oven. Let cool fully.

2. Core cooled ice cream cone cupcakes.

3. Remove ice cream from freezer just before serving. Ice cream needs to be very firm. Slide corer along the top of the ice cream, to ensure you get all flavors (if using Neapolitan ice cream). Slide ice cream out of corer into cupcake cone.

4. Top with whipped cream and serve immediately with your favorite toppings.

TIP: If making ahead for a party, simply freeze the ice cream-stuffed cupcake cone until ready to serve. Top immediately before serving with whipped cream, or let your guests do their own.

Cannoli Cream Stuffed Cupcakes

Makes 18 cupcakes

BASE
1 chocolate cake box mix
Eggs, oil & water *(per box directions)*

FILLING
Homemade Cannoli Cream Filling
1 c. ricotta cheese
2 c. powdered sugar
1/2 tsp. almond extract
1/2 c. cream cheese, whipped
1/2 c. mini chocolate chips

TOPPING
2 cans vanilla frosting
1/2 c. mini chocolate chips
1 box butter crisp cookies
  OR 1 waffle cone, in pieces
1/2 c. powdered sugar, for dusting

INSTRUCTIONS
1. Prepare chocolate cupcakes per box directions, **but only bake for 18 minutes.** Insert a toothpick to check for doneness; when it comes out clean, remove from oven. Let cool fully.

2. *While cupcakes bake, prepare filling:*
Cream together ricotta cheese, powdered sugar, almond extract and cream cheese. Using a spatula, stir mini chocolate chips into mixture. Place mixture in filling bag containing no tip. Set aside.

3. Core cupcakes. Cut a 1/2-inch hole from corner of filling bag and fill cupcakes.

4. Insert 1M tip into chosen pastry bag. Fill bag with plain vanilla frosting, cut opening and circle frost cupcakes.

5. Place half of a butter crisp cookie or piece of waffle cone on top of each cupcake. Sprinkle with mini chocolate chips and dust with powdered sugar.

Blueberry Sour Cream Stuffed Cupcakes

Makes 18 cupcakes

BASE
1 lemon cake box mix
Eggs & oil *(per box directions)*
Sour cream *(replaces water, ratio 1:1)*

FILLING
Homemade Blueberry Filling
1/2 c. blueberries
2 Tbsp. water
1/8 c. sugar
1 Tbsp. corn starch
   OR *1 (21 oz.) can blueberry pie filling*

TOPPING
2 cans vanilla frosting
Zest of 2 lemons *(1 lemon per can of frosting)*
Fresh or frozen blueberries
White sparkling sugar

INSTRUCTIONS
1. Replace all water in box mix directions with sour cream. Then prepare lemon cupcakes per box directions, **but only bake for 18 minutes.** Insert a toothpick to check for doneness; when it comes out clean, remove from oven. Let cool fully.

2. *While cupcakes bake, prepare filling & frosting:*
Filling: Dissolve corn starch into water. Place mixture in a saucepan on medium heat with the blueberries and sugar. Heat for 5-10 minutes and stir occasionally, until thickened. Set aside to cool. Once cool, place mixture into filling bag containing no tip. Set aside.
Frosting: Stir zest into the vanilla frosting. Insert 1M tip into chosen pastry bag. Fill bag with lemon-vanilla frosting.

3. Core cooled cupcakes. Cut a 1/2-inch hole from corner of filling bag and fill cupcakes. Cut opening in frosting bag, and circle frost cupcakes.

4. Sprinkle with white sparkling sugar and top with fresh or frozen blueberries.

The Metz family picked these beautiful blueberries. Oregon is blanketed with U-Pick farms, which is why it's so hard for us to travel anywhere else during July and August. We even bought an upright freezer so that we could preserve the harvest and enjoy it year-round.
♥ Julie

Fourth of July Mini-Pies

Makes 2 lattice-topped or 4 cut-out topped mini-pies

My dad was an amazing pie maker. He even taught classes on pie making at our church. I tried to duplicate some of his techniques with our own mini-pies. I think he would've liked to have made these mini-pies with me. ♥ Holly

CHERRY-ALMOND MINI-PIES

BASE
1 box refrigerated pie dough
  (containing 2 rolled dough sheets)

CHERRY- ALMOND FILLING
1 (21 oz.) can cherry pie filling
2 tsp. almond extract

TOPPING
1/4 c. milk *(optional)*
White sparkling sugar

INSTRUCTIONS

1. Bring refrigerated pie dough to room temperature, about 20 minutes.

2. *While pie dough is resting, prepare filling:*
Open the can of cherry pie filling. Add 2 tsp. of almond extract directly into the can, and stir.

3. Open package of pie dough, and unroll into two flat sheets. Using a 4" round cookie cutter or a 4" glass, cut out four circles per sheet of pie dough.

4. Place one 4" circle in a muffin cup opening and gently press down into the cup using your thumbs. Stretch the dough just enough to have about a 1/2" lip on the tray. Leave a muffin cup empty between pies to allow room for top crusts.

5. Fill with pie filling until gently mounding.

6. Using second sheet of pie dough, follow lattice instructions. *(See page 71.)*

7. Once the lattice is done, gently press down on dough (so it doesn't fall apart), and cut a 4" circle out of the lattice pie dough. Place 4" lattice circle on top of cherry pie filling. Pinch top pie crust to bottom using your index fingers, firmly securing top and bottom together.

8. Paint the top of your pie with milk (for sheen), and sprinkle with white sparkling sugar. Bake at 425 degrees for 15-18 minutes, or until top crust is lightly browned.

9. Remove from oven and let cool. Gently slide a sharp knife under edge of crust to loosen it from the pan, and then lift pie from muffin cup.

LATTICE INSTRUCTIONS

1. Cut pie dough into long strips, 1/2" wide. Fold every other vertical strip back towards you, almost in half. Lay a piece of pie dough across the strips horizontally and then fold pie dough back over the horizontal strip you just laid down.

2. Next, fold back the vertical strips that haven't been folded back yet, over the horizontal piece you just laid down. Place another horizontal piece down and fold vertical strips back.

3. Continue to do this until all pie dough is woven.

PART 1

PART 2

Download a free QR code reader app on your cell phone to access our video instructions.

BLUEBERRY-ORANGE MINI-PIES

BASE
1 box refrigerated pie dough
   (containing 2 rolled dough sheets)

BLUEBERRY-ORANGE FILLING
1 (21 oz.) can blueberry pie filling
2 Tbsp. orange juice
1 Tbsp. sugar

TOPPING
1/4 c. milk
White sparkling sugar

See facing page for step-by-step instructions on how these mini-crusts are made.

INSTRUCTIONS
1. Bring refrigerated pie dough to room temperature, about 20 minutes.

2. *While pie dough is resting, prepare filling:*
Open the can of blueberry pie filling. Add orange juice and sugar directly into the can, and stir.

3. Open package of pie dough and unroll into two flat sheets. Using a 4" round cookie cutter or a 4" glass, cut out 4 circles from each sheet of pie dough.

4. Place one 4" circle in a muffin pan opening and gently press down into the cup using your thumbs. Stretch the dough just enough to have a 1/2" lip on the tray. Leave a muffin cup empty between pies to allow room for top crusts.

5. Fill with pie filling until gently mounding.

6. Take another pre-cut 4" circle of pie dough and, using a small cookie cutter, cut out a shape to vent pie and to make decorative. Place vented 4" circle on top of blueberry-orange pie filling in muffin cup. Pinch top pie crust to bottom using your index fingers, firmly securing top and bottom together.

7. Paint the top of your pie with milk (for sheen), and sprinkle with white sparkling sugar. Bake at 425 degrees for 15-18 minutes, or until top crust is lightly browned.

8. Remove from oven and let cool. Gently slide a sharp knife under edge of crust to loosen it from the pan, and then lift pie from muffin cup.

Using a 4" diameter cup, cut 4 circles from each sheet of pie dough.

Fill with pie filling until gently mounding.
Use a small cookie cutter to cut out a shape, vent pie and make decorative.
Place vented 4" circle on top of blueberry-orange pie filling in muffin cup.

Pinch top pie crust to bottom, firmly securing top and bottom together.
Paint the top of your pie with milk, and sprinkle with white sparkling sugar.

Butterscotch Pineapple Mini-Cakes

Makes 18 mini-cakes

BASE
1 yellow cake box mix
Eggs, oil & water *(per box directions)*
1 c. butterscotch chips *(optional)*

FILLING
1 c. butterscotch chips
1 Tbsp. shortening
18 maraschino cherries, no stems
1 can pineapple chunks

TOPPING
Powdered sugar

Photo by Holly Haber

INSTRUCTIONS
1. Prepare yellow cake batter according to box directions, adding 1 c. butterscotch chips (if you choose). Set aside.

2. *Prepare filling:*
Place 1 c. of butterscotch chips and shortening into a microwave-safe bowl. Microwave on high for about 1 minute. Remove and stir until smooth. If chips aren't completely melted, microwave additional 30 seconds.

3. Coat muffin pan with cooking spray. Spoon the melted butterscotch mixture into muffin tin, just enough to cover the bottom.

4. Place cherry into the center of the butterscotch mixture and then place 4 halved chunks of pineapple into each muffin cup, making a flower shape *(as shown)*. Spoon butterscotch chip cake batter on top of pineapple/cherry/butterscotch layer, until two-thirds full. **Bake for 18 minutes.** Check for doneness with a toothpick.

5. Remove from oven, and **immediately** turn mini-cakes upside down onto waxed paper or a foil-lined pan to prevent sticking. Let cool fully.

6. Garnish with sifted powdered sugar.

Every year on his birthday, my husband wants one of two cakes: an Upside-Down Cake or a Rum Cake. Over the years, I have massacred both, but when I found a recipe for a Butterscotch Pineapple Upside-Down Cake, we hit the jackpot.

This is an easier version of that recipe and the first time I've tried the miniature version – I'll never go back!! Previously, half of the butterscotch, pineapples & cherries stayed stuck in the bottom of a cast iron skillet. Why is that you ask? Because I was trying to invert a pan that weighed 20 pounds and was the temperature of the sun!

With this easy recipe, I'm done in less than an half hour; they all popped right out of the pan, and everyone gets their own mini-cake.

♥ Holly

Cake Pops

Makes 25 cake pops

BASE
1 cake box mix, any flavor
   (baked, per box directions)
1/4 can frosting
25 lollipop sticks

DIPPING CHOCOLATE
2 c. white chocolate chips
2 Tbsp. shortening

TOPPING
Rainbow sprinkles
White sparkling sugar

TIP: What can you do with all your extra cupcake cores? Take 18 cores leftover from any of our recipes, add 3 tsp. vanilla frosting and follow instructions below. Makes 3. (If you want enough for a party, follow the full recipe.)

INSTRUCTIONS

1. Crumble cooled cake into fine crumbs, using a fork.

2. Add a quarter can of frosting and mix well with the back of a spoon until all cake is completely combined and sticking together, like cookie dough. Roll dough into a ball, about the size of a walnut, or use a 1-inch cookie scoop. Set aside. Finish making balls with the remainder of dough.

3. Place white chocolate chips and shortening in a microwave-safe bowl, and heat on high for 30 seconds. Stir. Microwave another 30 seconds, and stir until smooth. If not completely melted, continue microwaving in 15-second increments.

4. Dip lollipop stick into white chocolate and insert into formed cake ball; when hardened, it helps prevent the stick from sliding out. Dip newly formed cake pop into the melted white chocolate. Use a spoon to drizzle over inverted pop to completely cover, if desired.

5. Once coated, twist cake pop as you raise it out of the bowl, to drain off excess white chocolate. Immediately sprinkle with garnish.

6. You may place completed cake pops, stick side down, in a mug or foam block to allow white chocolate to harden.

Photos by Holly Haber

Cookie Dough Stuffed Cupcakes

Makes 18 Cupcakes

BASE
1 chocolate cake box mix
Eggs, oil & water *(per box directions)*

HOMEMADE FILLING
3/4 c. granulated sugar
3/4 c. dark brown sugar
1 c. butter, softened
1½ Tbsp. vanilla extract
2 c. flour
3 Tbsp. water
1 c. mini chocolate chips

TOPPING
2 cans chocolate frosting
Mini chocolate chips, jimmies,
    rainbow-coated chocolates,
    mini chocolate chip cookies

INSTRUCTIONS
1. Prepare chocolate cupcakes per box directions, **but only bake for 18 minutes.** Insert a toothpick to check for doneness; when it comes out clean, remove from oven. Let cool fully.

2. Core cooled cupcakes and insert rolled cookie dough. *(See facing page.)*

3. Insert 1M tip into chosen pastry bag. Fill bag with chocolate frosting, cut opening and circle frost cupcakes.

4. Top cupcakes with your favorite topping, or use all four!

If working on your back-to-school to-do list has you needing a bit of comfort, sneak a gob of this cookie dough when no one is looking. The filling in our Cookie Dough Stuffed Cupcakes contains no eggs, so sample away – if you like that sort of thing!

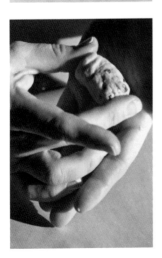

FILLING
Homemade Cookie Dough Filling

1. Cream sugars, softened butter, vanilla and water together with electric mixer.

2. Slowly add flour into sugar mixture while mixing with beaters.

3. Using a spatula, stir mini-chocolate chips into mixture.

4. Roll into 1-inch-wide by 2-inch-long logs.

Oatmeal Toffee Scotchie Bars & Cookies

Makes 9 bars & 1 dozen cookies

OATMEAL TOFFEE SCOTCHIE BARS

BAR BASE
1 blondie bar pouch mix
Eggs, butter & water *(per box directions)*

FILLING
1 oatmeal cookie pouch mix
2 Tbsp. vanilla extract
1/2 (8 oz.) bag of toffee chips
1/2 (11 oz.) bag of butterscotch chips

INSTRUCTIONS
1. Prepare blondie batter per package instructions, and then divide in half. Press half into the bottom of a greased 8 x 8 pan.

2. *Prepare filling:*
Mix oatmeal cookie dough per package instructions. Once completely combined, mix in butterscotch chips, toffee chips and vanilla extract.

3. Layer half of the oatmeal cookie batter filling over the blondie batter mix in the bottom of pan. Top with the final layer of blondie batter mix, and bake for 40 minutes at 350 degrees. Insert a toothpick to check for doneness; when it comes out clean, remove from oven. Let cool fully.

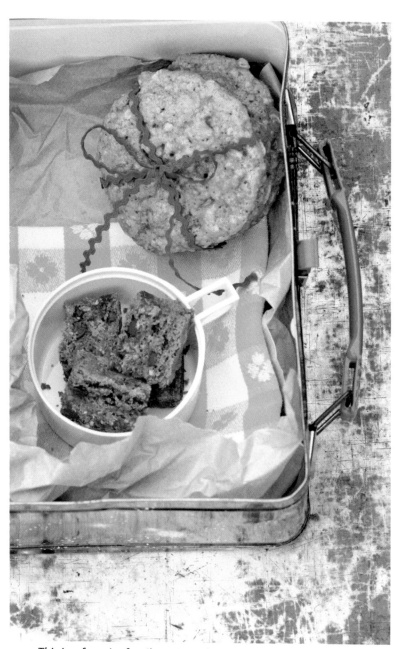

This is a favorite family recipe. There will be filling left over after the bars are stuffed, so I make Oatmeal Toffee Scotchie Cookies, two desserts in one – you're welcome! ♥ Holly

OATMEAL TOFFEE SCOTCHIE COOKIES

COOKIE BASE
1 oatmeal cookie pouch mix
Eggs, butter & water *(per box directions)*

FILLING
2 Tbsp. vanilla extract
1/2 (8 oz.) bag of toffee chips
1/2 (11 oz.) bag of butterscotch chips

Use the remaining filling from the blondie bars (facing page) to make the cookies, or follow these instructions if not making both recipes during your baking session:

INSTRUCTIONS
1. Mix oatmeal cookie batter according to package directions. Add in vanilla extract, toffee chips and butterscotch chips. Stir to combine.

2. Using a small batter scoop, portion cookie mixture onto parchment-lined cookie sheet.

3. Bake cookies at 350 degrees for 10-13 minutes.

4. Remove from oven and let cool.

Cookies & Cream Stuffed Cupcakes

Makes 18 Cupcakes

BASE
1 chocolate cake box mix
Eggs, oil & water *(per box directions)*

FILLING
1 can vanilla frosting
1 package chocolate sandwich cookies

TOPPING
2 cans vanilla frosting
Crushed chocolate sandwich cookies
1/2 chocolate sandwich cookie, per cupcake

INSTRUCTIONS
1. Prepare chocolate cupcakes per box directions, **but only bake for 18 minutes.** Insert toothpick to check for doneness; when it comes out clean, remove from oven. Let cool.

2. *While cupcakes bake, prepare filling:*
Place half package chocolate sandwich cookies into a large bowl. Using a potato masher, crush cookies into smaller pieces (approx. 1/2" size). Add 1 can of vanilla frosting to crushed cookies and stir to combine. Place mixture in filling bag containing no tip. Set aside.

3. Core cooled cupcakes. Cut a **1-inch hole** from corner of filling bag and fill cupcakes.

4. Insert 1M tip into chosen pastry bag. Fill bag with plain vanilla frosting, cut opening and circle frost cupcakes.

5. Finely chop four cookies. Sprinkle over frosted cupcakes; add half a cookie on top.

To prevent cookies from cracking unevenly, use a sharp knife and chop quickly through them.

Fall

Rhubarb-Stuffed Sweet Potato Muffins

Makes 12 muffins

BASE
1 (14 oz.) Sweet potato muffin mix
Eggs, oil & water *(per box directions)*
1/2 tsp. brown sugar, per muffin

FILLING
Homemade Rhubarb Filling
2 c. fresh rhubarb, chopped 1/2"
pieces
1/4 c. granulated sugar
1/4 c. orange juice
1/2 c. water
1 Tbsp. raspberry instant jello

TOPPING
12 tsp. plain Greek yogurt

INSTRUCTIONS
1. Prepare and bake sweet potato muffins per box directions. Fill two-thirds full and sprinkle with brown sugar before baking. Insert a toothpick to check for doneness; when it comes out clean, remove from oven. Let cool.

2. *While muffins bake, prepare filling:*
Place filling ingredients in a saucepan and heat 7-10 minutes on medium-high heat, hot enough to simmer, stirring often. Remove from heat to cool.

3. Core cooled muffins and fill with one heaping teaspoon of the rhubarb compote.

4. When completely cooled, garnish with Greek yogurt and additional rhubarb sauce, to taste.

I was inspired by a Southern rhubarb dump cake for this recipe. When I couldn't find an oatmeal muffin mix at my local grocery store, I grudgingly got the sweet potato muffin mix. I just didn't want to drive one more place to find a different box mix! Luckily for me, the earthy sweet potato flavor ended up being a perfect fit for these Rhubarb-Stuffed Sweet Potato Muffins. My daughters also were skeptics when I tried to sell them on the flavors for their after-school snack, but they ended up loving it. "I could live off this filling, mom," one said. Me, too. Enjoy with a cup of coffee.
♥ Julie

Peppermint Cream Stuffed Cupcakes

Makes 18 cupcakes

BASE
1 chocolate cake box mix
Eggs, oil & water *(per box directions)*

FILLING
Homemade Peppermint Cream Filling
2 c. powdered sugar
1/4 tsp. peppermint extract
1/4 tsp. vanilla extract
2 tsp. butter, softened
2 Tbsp. milk

TOPPING
2 cans chocolate frosting
1 bag peppermint-coated chocolates
White sugar pearls

INSTRUCTIONS
1. Prepare chocolate cupcakes per box directions, **but only bake for 18 minutes.** Insert a toothpick to check for doneness; when it comes out clean, remove from oven. Let cool fully.

2. *While cupcakes bake, prepare filling:* Cream together powdered sugar, peppermint & vanilla extracts, milk and butter. Roll into 2-inch-long logs.

3. Core cooled cupcakes and insert filling.

4. Insert 1M tip into chosen pastry bag. Fill bag with chocolate frosting, cut opening and circle frost cupcakes.

5. Top with pearls and quartered candies.

We count Army, Navy and Marine Corps veterans among our family members, who served in the Revolutionary War, World Wars I & II, the Vietnam War and the Gulf War. Thanks to them and all of you who serve, our freedom stands on the shoulders of giants.

TIP: If peppermint filling isn't firm enough to roll, add more powdered sugar.

Peanut Butter Stuffed Cupcakes

Makes 18 cupcakes

BASE
1 chocolate cake box mix
Eggs, oil & water *(per box directions)*

FILLING
Homemade Peanut Butter Filling
1 c. peanut butter
2 c. powdered sugar
2 Tbsp. vanilla extract

TOPPING
2 cans chocolate frosting
18 mini peanut butter cups
Crumbled filling
Chocolate jimmies

INSTRUCTIONS

1. Prepare chocolate cupcakes per box directions, **but only bake for 18 minutes.** Insert a toothpick to check for doneness; when it comes out clean, remove from oven. Let cool fully.

2. *While cupcakes bake, prepare the filling:*
Beat together filling ingredients and form into 1-inch-wide by 2-inch-long logs.

3. Core cooled cupcakes and insert filling.

4. Insert 1M tip into chosen pastry bag. Fill bag with chocolate frosting, cut opening and circle frost cupcakes.

5. Garnish with PB cups, crumbled filling or jimmies.

Chai Latte Stuffed Cupcakes

Makes 18 cupcakes

BASE
1 vanilla cake box mix
Eggs & oil *(per box directions)*
1 c. chai tea, liquid concentrate

FILLING
1½ c. milk
1 (5.1 oz.) vanilla
          instant pudding

TOPPING
1 (12 oz.) tub whipped topping
Grated cinnamon
Grated nutmeg
Cinnamon stick *(garnish only)*

Start on side of the cupcake, and while applying pressure to bag, zigzag across the top of the cupcake. For a leaf effect, draw a line bisecting the whipped topping with a toothpick.

INSTRUCTIONS
1. Replace all water in box mix directions with chai tea. Then prepare vanilla cupcakes per box directions, **but only bake for 18 minutes.** Insert a toothpick to check for doneness; when it comes out clean, remove from oven. Let cool fully.

2. *While cupcakes bake, prepare filling:*
In a mixing bowl, prepare vanilla pudding using just 1½ c. of milk to make a thicker pudding. Refrigerate filling until cupcakes are completely cooled.

3. Core cooled cupcakes and insert filling with a spoon until slightly mounded.

4. Fill chosen pastry bag with whipped topping, then cut a 1/2-inch hole from corner of bag. Start on side of the cupcake; while applying pressure to bag, zigzag across the top of the cupcake. For a leaf effect, draw a line bisecting the whipped topping with a toothpick.

5. Sprinkle or grate fresh cinnamon and/or nutmeg on top. If you sprinkle too much, simply blow off the extra. Garnish with a quarter stick of cinnamon, if desired.

If living in the Pacific Northwest a dozen years has taught me anything, it's lattes, baby. Tea and coffee taste better (to me!) with milk, half-n-half, cream, soy milk, etc. I love the bold spice profile of chai. ♥ Julie

Black Forest Stuffed Cupcakes
Makes 18 cupcakes

This decadent cherry-stuffed cupcake is a must-make. The chocolate curls add to its richness; you won't believe how easy they are to make. All you need is a vegetable peeler and a chocolate bar.

BASE
1 chocolate cake box mix
Eggs, oil & water *(per box directions)*

FILLING
1 (21 oz.) can cherry pie filling
1 tsp. almond extract

TOPPING
2 cans chocolate fudge frosting
1 milk chocolate bar
1 (10 oz.) jar maraschino cherries

INSTRUCTIONS
1. Prepare chocolate cupcakes per box directions, **but only bake for 18 minutes.** Insert a toothpick to check for doneness; when it comes out clean, remove from oven. Let cool fully.

2. *While cupcakes bake, prepare filling*: Mix almond extract into can of cherry pie filling.

3. Core cooled cupcakes and insert cherry filling with a spoon until slightly mounded.

4. Insert 1M tip into chosen pastry bag. Fill bag with chocolate frosting, cut opening and circle frost cupcakes.

5. Sprinkle cupcake with chocolate curls & place a cherry on top.

HOW TO CURL CHOCOLATE
Unwrap your favorite chocolate bar. Use a vegetable peeler to curl the chocolate down the long edge of the bar. The warmer the bar, the longer and thicker the curl with be. However, you may need to periodically refrigerate the bar so that it doesn't melt in your hand.

German Chocolate Stuffed Cupcakes

Makes 18 cupcakes

Toasted coconut gives another layer of texture to this rich chocolate cupcake. I just love the way the filling mounds up on top... you get a sneak peek of what's inside. ♥ *Holly*

TOASTING COCONUT
Place sweetened coconut onto a parchment-lined pan and toast for 3-5 minutes. Stir the coconut with a spoon, and continue toasting until golden brown.
Set aside to cool.

BASE
1 chocolate cake box mix
Eggs, oil & water *(per box directions)*

FILLING
2 cans coconut pecan frosting

TOPPING
2 cans chocolate frosting
2 c. sweetened coconut, toasted

INSTRUCTIONS
1. Prepare chocolate cupcakes per box directions, **but only bake for 18 minutes.** Insert a toothpick to check for doneness; when it comes out clean, remove from oven. Let cool fully.

2. *While cupcakes bake, prepare filling:* Insert 1M tip into chosen pastry bag. Fill bag with coconut pecan filling and cut opening.

3. Core cooled cupcakes and pipe in filling.

4. Insert another 1M tip into a second pastry bag. Fill bag with chocolate frosting, and cut an opening. Pipe one circle around the coconut pecan filling. Add more filling so it mounds up above the frosting. *(See photo.)*

5. Toast coconut. Gather small amount of toasted coconut in palm and pat in a circle around the chocolate frosting's outer edge.

93

Pumpkin Chocolate Stuffed Cupcakes

Makes 18 cupcakes

BASE
1 spice cake box mix
1 (14 oz.) can of pumpkin

BAKED-IN FILLING
*Homemade Chocolate
 Cream Cheese Filling*
2 Tbsp. unsweetened cocoa
8 oz. cream cheese
1/4 c. powdered sugar
1 egg
1/8 tsp. salt

TOPPING
2 cans cream cheese frosting
Raw sugar

Pumpkin puree is a healthier substitute for oil and water in this recipe, creating dense, spice-filled stuffed cupcakes.

INSTRUCTIONS
Do not *add any of the ingredients listed on the box mix.*

1. Empty the dry spice box mix into a bowl and add one can of pumpkin puree. Mix together completely. The batter will be very thick. Set aside.

2. *Prepare filling:*
In a separate bowl, with a mixer, cream together cocoa, cream cheese, powdered sugar, egg and salt. Mixture will be slightly lumpy.

3. Scoop batter into cupcake liners using an cookie scoop. Make a deep well in the center of scooped batter with the back of a spoon sprayed with cooking spray. Then fill centers with 1 tsp. filling mixture.

4. Place in oven and cook for 15 minutes. Remove from oven. Leave in pan for 5 minutes to let cupcakes finishing cooking. Remove and cool completely.

5. Insert 1M tip into chosen pastry bag. Fill bag with plain cream cheese frosting, cut opening and circle frost cupcakes.

6. Sprinkle with raw sugar.

Julie and I were talking about how excited we were that it was fall because of all the pumpkin items that are now available. She told me that each year, her out-of-state sisters spend an afternoon together shopping for (and tasting!) pumpkin-flavored treats. What a great fall tradition!

Coconut Caramel Stuffed Cupcakes

Makes 18 cupcakes

BASE
1 yellow cake box mix
Eggs, oil & water *(per box directions)*

FILLING
1 (17 oz.) jar butterscotch
        caramel topping
          (found in the ice cream aisle)

TOPPING
2 cans chocolate frosting
1/2 c. sweetened coconut, toasted
1 package chocolate, coconut
  & caramel-flavored cookies

Toast coconut until it's golden brown before sprinkling onto the finished cupcakes. But watch it like a hawk... it burns easily.

INSTRUCTIONS

1. Prepare yellow cupcakes per box directions, **but only bake for 18 minutes.** Insert a toothpick to check for doneness; when it comes out clean, remove from oven. Let cool fully.

2. *While cupcakes bake, prepare topping:*
Place coconut onto a metal tray and toast in a toaster oven 3-5 minutes. Stir the coconut with a spoon, and toast another few minutes or until golden brown. Set aside to cool.

3. Core cooled cupcakes. Fill each cored cupcake with 1 Tbsp. butterscotch caramel topping per cupcake.

4. Insert 1M tip into chosen pastry bag. Fill bag with chocolate frosting, cut opening and circle frost cupcakes.

5. Sprinkle toasted coconut onto each cupcake. With a sharp knife, cut the store-bought cookie into quarters, and place one piece on top of decorated cupcake.

Every year for the past 14, I've volunteered at day camp with my daughters. Because it's a volunteer-run camp, there is a Thank you Tea. This year, I provided cupcakes to go along with the beautiful meal that my friend Angie and her daughter, Kayla, prepared. Of course, being a scouting event, the cupcakes were themed! I got some rave reviews about these cupcakes.
♥ Holly

97

Cranberry Orange Stuffed Cupcakes

Makes 18 cupcakes

BASE
1 orange cake box mix
Eggs, oil & water *(per box directions)*

FILLING *(See facing page.)*
Homemade Cranberry Orange Filling
   OR *Time-Saver Cranberry Orange Filling*

TOPPING
1 (12 oz.) tub whipped topping, thawed
Fresh cranberries
Baker's sugar or granulated
Walnuts, chopped
White sparkling sugar

INSTRUCTIONS
1. Prepare orange cupcakes per box directions, **but only bake for 18 minutes.** Insert a toothpick to check for doneness; when it comes out clean, remove from oven. Let cool fully.

2. Core cooled cupcakes and insert cranberry orange filling with a spoon until slightly mounded. *(See facing page.)*

3. Insert 1M tip into chosen pastry bag. Fill bag with whipped topping, cut opening and circle frost cupcakes.

5. *Prepare garnish:*
Place fresh cranberries in a colander and rinse. While cranberries are still damp, roll in Baker's sugar.

6. Garnish with a sugared cranberry, a piece of walnut and white sparkling sugar.

If you don't have Baker's sugar on hand, roll the cranberries in granulated sugar.
If you want to make your own Baker's sugar, here's how: Place 1/2 cup of granulated sugar into a food processor or grinder; grind for about 20 seconds or until sugar is a finer consistency.

FILLING

Homemade Cranberry Orange Filling
1 c. sugar
1 c. fresh cranberries
Zest of 1 naval orange
1 naval orange, peeled and cut into bite-sized pieces
1/2 c. walnuts
1/2 c. water
1 Tbsp. cornstarch
1 Tbsp. water

1. Combine sugar, cranberries, zest, navel orange, walnuts and water in a saucepan.

2. Cook over medium heat for 5 minutes, stirring occasionally.

3. In a separate bowl, combine cornstarch and water until completely dissolved. Pour cornstarch mixture into cranberry-orange mixture and continue to cook for 3 minutes.

4. Remove from heat and let cool fully.

OR

Time-saver Cranberry Orange Filling
1 (14 oz.) can of cranberry sauce
3/4 c. orange marmalade
1/2 c. walnuts

1. Place can of cranberry sauce, orange marmalade and walnuts in a saucepan.

2. Heat over medium heat for about 5 minutes or until heated through. Heating the ingredients helps blend the flavors.

3. Remove from heat and let cool fully.

Persimmon Thumbprint Cookies

Makes 30 cookies

BASE

Mom's Honey Pecan Balls
1 c. butter (2 sticks)
1 c. shortening
8 Tbsp. honey
4 c. sifted flour
1/2 tsp. salt
2 tsp. vanilla extract
2 c. finely chopped pecans
Powdered sugar *for dusting*
   OR *2 packages snickerdoodle
   cookie mix (per box directions)*

FILLING *(See page 103.)*
Homemade Persimmon Filling

If you don't own a sifter, combine dry ingredients in a separate bowl using a whisk. We used a food processor on the pecans.

INSTRUCTIONS

You may substitute 2 snickerdoodle cookie mixes for the base. However, these will spread more when baking than in the homemade version. Prepare cookie mix according to package directions, and skip to filling, page 103.

1. With a mixer, cream the butter and shortening with the honey and vanilla extract until well-combined.

2. In a separate bowl, sift flour and salt together. Combine with butter mixture. Use stand mixer to combine, as this is a thick batter. Stir in the chopped pecans.

3. Using a medium cookie scoop (about 2 Tbsp.), scoop 12 to 15 cookies onto a baking sheet. Press a well into the center with your thumb.

4. Once your persimmon filling is made, fill the well with 1 tsp. of the jam.

5. Bake for 16 minutes at 335 degrees. Remove from oven when the bottom edges of the cookies turn golden brown.

6. Let the cookies rest for 2 minutes on the baking sheet before moving them to a cooling rack.

This stuffed cookie recipe is the marriage of my mom's Honey Pecan Balls – a Christmas favorite from her Aunt Marie similar to Mexican Wedding Cookies and my neighbor's organic Fuyu persimmons, when they produced last fall. The filling's flavor is similar to baked peaches. It also has a slight squash undertone, which pairs well with the pecans and nutmeg of the butter cookie base.
♥ Julie

HOW TO BREAK DOWN A PERSIMMON

Ripened fruit is mostly orange and cracks around the top stem base, similar to a tomato.

1. Turn the fruit stem-side down and cut partway through the center, stopping just before the leaf stem.

2. Pull apart the persimmon and stem with a bit of the core, much like hulling a strawberry.

3. Quarter the fruit and peel the skin off with a paring knife or vegetable peeler. Cut the fruit into a medium dice for heating.

These beautiful thumbprint cookies were made using our persimmon filling and a store-bought snickerdoodle mix.

FILLING

Homemade Persimmon Filling

4 Fuyu persimmons,
   peeled & diced
1 Tbsp. water
3 whole cloves
1 tsp. lemon juice
1/4 c. granulated sugar
1/8 tsp. nutmeg

Store-bought peach jam is a comparable filling.

INSTRUCTIONS

1. Place diced persimmons and water in a medium-sized saucepan over medium-high heat.

2. Add in cloves, lemon juice, sugar and nutmeg. Cook for about 7 minutes, stirring occasionally.

3. Remove the three cloves and dispose of them.

4. Remove from heat when the fruit is a jam-like consistency. Use a stick blender or food processor to blend if you prefer a smoother consistency.

Dutch Apple Pie Muffins

Makes 12 muffins

BASE

1 cinnamon streusel muffin mix
  If your mix does not include a streusel topping, make
  Brown Sugar Crumble recipe (See page 106.)
Eggs, oil & water *(per box directions)*

FILLING

1 (20 oz.) can apple pie filling

TOPPING

Pie dough cutouts *(See page 107.)*
Cheddar cheese

INSTRUCTIONS

1. Prepare and bake cinnamon streusel muffins according to box directions. Fill muffin cups two-thirds full and sprinkle with brown sugar crumble before baking. (If your box mix doesn't contain streusel topping, use the recipe page 106). Cover brown sugar mixture with another small scoop of batter and sprinkle with the remaining brown sugar; don't press down.

2. Bake for about 25 minutes at 350 degrees. Insert a toothpick to check for doneness; when it comes out clean, remove from oven. Let cool fully.

3. *While muffins bake, prepare filling:*
Open apple pie filling and cut the canned apples into 1/2" pieces. Set aside.

4. Core cooled muffins and fill with prepared apple pie filling.

5. Place baked pie cutout *(page 107)* upright on top of the muffin and add a small cube of cheese.

If you intentionally over-sprinkle the sugar on your pie dough cutout, it will caramelize and form a beautiful amber-stained sugar glass. Just remember to use a parchment-lined baking sheet for easier removal.

105

TOPPING
Make this topping from scratch if it's not already included in your box mix.

Homemade Brown Sugar Crumble
1 cup packed light brown sugar
1 cup all-purpose flour
1 tsp. ground cinnamon
1/2 stick of butter (cut into cubes and soften, or melt)

INSTRUCTIONS
1.Mix dry ingredients with a fork, and then mash in the butter until mixture is crumbly.

2. Add to center and top of muffin before baking.

ABOUT THAT CHEDDAR
My mom used to serve apple pie for breakfast from time to time when I was a kid. I always felt like I was getting away with something when she did this. She would justify it by serving it with a slice of cheddar cheese, so we had our protein and our fruit.

So, we've reinvented an old favorite as a stuffed muffin for a quick morning treat to enjoy during the holiday season! You can add raisins and nuts to include even more fruit and protein - justify it anyway you want! They're best served warm, with a slice of cheese. ♥ Holly

Oh, my gosh, Holly! I've never met anyone else who liked cheddar cheese with apple pie! My dad most always eats his apple pie with a slice of cheddar cheese melting on top; he says that's how his dad ate it. (Is it an Irish thing?) So, here we've added a bite-sized chunk. The saltiness of the cheese adds a nice depth of flavor. I'm sold.

And by the way, doesn't calling it a muffin instead of a cupcake make it a breakfast food? ♥ Julie

PIE DOUGH CUTOUTS

1. Using a small seasonal cookie cutter, cut out several shapes in the refrigerated pie douagh.

2. Place cutout on parchment-lined pan.

3. Brush pie dough with milk or a raw beaten egg.

4. Sprinkle with cinnamon sugar and bake until golden brown, about 5 minutes. However, you'll want to check them frequently. As soon as they start browning around the edges, remove them from the oven. Let cool fully.

Black Friday Stuffin' Muffins

Makes 12 muffins

BASE
1 stuffing box mix
   OR *leftover Thanksgiving stuffing*
2/3 c. half-n-half

FILLING
Homemade Egg Filling
2 Tbsp. butter
4 oz. mushrooms, chopped
6 eggs, beaten
1 tsp. salt
1 c. precooked sausage crumbles

TOPPING
1 ½ c. shredded cheese
Sliced green onion
Hot sauce, to taste

INSTRUCTIONS
1. Cook stuffing mix according to package directions. Set aside to cool.

2. Mix cooked stuffing with half-n-half to bind it, even if using leftover stuffing.

3. Line muffin tin with aluminum foil liners. Fill liners with stuffing mixture; using the back of a spoon, make a hole in the center of the mixture and press stuffing firmly against the sides of the muffin cups.

4. In another pan, sauté in butter and chopped mushrooms over med-high heat about 2 minutes. Add in beaten eggs, salt and sausage crumbles. Cook until soft scrambled.

5. Fill center of each muffin cup with egg filling, and top with shredded cheese.

6. Bake at 350 degrees for 35-40 minutes.

7. Garnish with shredded cheese, sliced green onion or hot sauce.

STUFFING BASE

EGG FILLING

We had the idea to use leftover Thanksgiving stuffing as base and then fill it with protein for a go-to Black Friday power muffin. We wanted it to be something you could throw together the night before and then grab and dash at say, 5 am? 3 am? My kids love these as an after-school snack, and named them Stuffin' Muffins.
♥ *Julie*

Maple Bacon Stuffed Cupcakes

Makes 18 cupcakes

BASE
1 butter yellow cake box mix
Eggs, oil & water *(per box directions)*

FILLING
1/4 c. maple syrup
1 can of butter cream frosting
1/4 tsp. salt

TOPPING
2 cans butter cream frosting

INSTRUCTIONS
1. Prepare butter yellow cupcakes per box directions, **but only bake for 18 minutes.** Insert a toothpick to check for doneness; when it comes out clean, remove from oven. Let cool fully.

2. *While cupcakes bake, prepare filling:* Combine 1 can of butter cream frosting with syrup and salt. Place mixture in filling bag containing no tip. Set aside.

3. Core cooled cupcakes. Cut a 1/2-inch hole from corner of filling bag and fill cupcakes.

4. Insert 1M tip into chosen pastry bag. Fill bag with plain butter cream frosting, cut opening and circle frost cupcakes.

5. Garnish cupcakes with cut up candied bacon; kitchen shears work well, but make sure bacon is cooled.

It's breakfast in a cupcake! These Maple Bacon Stuffed Cupcakes taste like the sweetest pancakes, with fantastic buttery syrup stuffed in the middle. Oh, yeah, and there's candied bacon on the top. YUM!!

CANDIED BACON

1/2 lb. bacon
1/3 c. brown sugar
2/3 c. syrup

INSTRUCTIONS
1. Line baking pan with foil; cut bacon in half.

2. Dredge bacon through syrup and then through brown sugar.

3. Place on pan and pat more sugar onto the bacon.

4. Bake in 400 degree oven for 20 to 25 minutes or until crispy and brown.

BEHIND THE SCENES

FLAVORS AND HOLIDAYS

INDEX

Scarlett

CPSIA information can be obtained at www.ICGtesting.com
Printed in the USA
BVIW12n0058300115
385613BV00001B/1